The 2022 Diary

ON THIS DAY IN HISTORY

Compiled and Edited by

Sarah Bingham

2022 CALENDAR

JANUARY

M	T	W	T	F	S	S
					1	2
3	4	5	6	7	8	9
10	11	12	13	14	15	16
17	18	19	20	21	22	23
24	25	26	27	28	29	30
31						

FEBRUARY

M	T	W	T	F	S	S
	1	2	3	4	5	6
7	8	9	10	11	12	13
14	15	16	17	18	19	20
21	22	23	24	25	26	27
28						

MARCH

M	T	W	T	F	S	S
	1	2	3	4	5	6
7	8	9	10	11	12	13
14	15	16	17	18	19	20
21	22	23	24	25	26	27
28	29	30	31			

APRIL

M	T	W	T	F	S	S
				1	2	3
4	5	6	7	8	9	10
11	12	13	14	15	16	17
18	19	20	21	22	23	24
25	26	27	28	29	30	

MAY

M	T	W	T	F	S	S
						1
2	3	4	5	6	7	8
9	10	11	12	13	14	15
16	17	18	19	20	21	22
23	24	25	26	27	28	29
30	31					

JUNE

M	T	W	T	F	S	S
		1	2	3	4	5
6	7	8	9	10	11	12
13	14	15	16	17	18	19
20	21	22	23	24	25	26
27	28	29	30			

JULY

M	T	W	T	F	S	S
				1	2	3
4	5	6	7	8	9	10
11	12	13	14	15	16	17
18	19	20	21	22	23	24
25	26	27	28	29	30	31

AUGUST

M	T	W	T	F	S	S
1	2	3	4	5	6	7
8	9	10	11	12	13	14
15	16	17	18	19	20	21
22	23	24	25	26	27	28
29	30	31				

SEPTEMBER

M	T	W	T	F	S	S
			1	2	3	4
5	6	7	8	9	10	11
12	13	14	15	16	17	18
19	20	21	22	23	24	25
26	27	28	29	30		

OCTOBER

M	T	W	T	F	S	S
					1	2
3	4	5	6	7	8	9
10	11	12	13	14	15	16
17	18	19	20	21	22	23
24	25	26	27	28	29	30
31						

NOVEMBER

M	T	W	T	F	S	S
	1	2	3	4	5	6
7	8	9	10	11	12	13
14	15	16	17	18	19	20
21	22	23	24	25	26	27
28	29	30				

DECEMBER

M	T	W	T	F	S	S
			1	2	3	4
5	6	7	8	9	10	11
12	13	14	15	16	17	18
19	20	21	22	23	24	25
26	27	28	29	30	31	

NOTES

NOTES

NOTES

On this day

1985

Dian Fossey, the American zoologist who was known as one of the world's foremost female scientists and conservationists, is found murdered in Rwanda. Her work has done a great deal to save mountain gorillas from extinction.

Monday 27th December 2021

On this day

1972

President Richard Nixon declares a day of mourning for the death of former President Harry S. Truman. As a result, 300 men are unable to answer their military drafts. The draft is not resumed in 1973, so these men are never sent to war.

Tuesday 28th December 2021

On this day

1170

Thomas Becket is assassinated inside Canterbury Cathedral by the knights of Henry II, although whether the king intended the archbishop's death remains uncertain. Becket has since become a martyr of both the Catholic and Anglican Church.

Wednesday 29th December 2021

Thursday 30th December 2021

On this day

1916

Russian mystic and royal advisor, Grigori Rasputin, is killed by tsarists who fear his influence over the crown. According to legend, he survives being poisoned, shot and bludgeoned before being placed in the Volga River.

Friday 31st December 2021

On this day

1759

Arthur Guinness takes out a 9,000 year lease on a brewery in St. James's Gate, Dublin, for an annual rent of £45. The drink which bears his name continues to be produced there today.

Sat 1st & Sun 2nd January 2022

On this day

1st January 1801

The Act of Union comes into effect, joining the Kingdoms of Great Britain and Ireland into the United Kingdom. A new flag known as the Union Jack is created, using the crosses of St. George, St. Andrew and St. Patrick.

Monday 3rd January 2022

Solomon Northup regains his freedom, twelve years after being kidnapped and sold into slavery. In the same year he publishes his memoir, *Twelve Years a Slave*, which becomes a bestseller.

Tuesday 4th January 2022

Danish barbers' assistants agree to return to work, 33 years after going on strike. The Guinness World Record for the world's longest recorded strike is still unbroken.

Wednesday 5th January 2022

Captain Alfred Dreyfus is sentenced to life imprisonment on Devil's Island for treason. Evidence of his innocence is suppressed. He is exonerated after 11 years, but remains a symbol of injustice and antisemitism in France.

Thursday 6th January 2022

Maria Montessori opens the first 'Casa dei Bambini' in a tenement block in Rome. Her educational methods, emphasising independent learning rather than teacher-led testing, have since spread throughout the world.

Friday 7th January 2022

Six days after it began, the Battle of Raate Road comes to an end. The 9th Division of Finland, numbering 6,000 men, earn a decisive victory over two Soviet divisions. Heavy Soviet losses during the Winter War contribute to Adolf Hitler's decision to invade in 1941.

Sat 8th & Sun 9th January 2022

The New York State Legislature passes a bill to prohibit public flirting. The first offence would be fined $25, while the second carried the punishment of being ordered to wear horse blinders when outdoors. This law still exists, but is rarely enforced.

Monday 10th January 2022

Thomas Paine anonymously publishes his *Common Sense* pamphlet, advocating American independence from Great Britain. It is highly influential in persuading the public towards revolution and remains one of the best-selling books in American history.

Tuesday 11th January 2022

Ten days after learning that a shortened work week brought with it a pay cut, workers at almost every mill in Lawrence, Massachusetts go on strike. The strike lasts for two months and unites female and immigrant workers of 51 nationalities, ending in a 20% pay raise.

Wednesday 12th January 2022

A storm prevents the crew of Lynmouth Lifeboat Station in Devon from launching to the rescue of a distressed ship. 20 men instead carry the lifeboat for 15 miles through a gale to Porlock Weir, a journey which takes 11 hours. The rescue is completed on 14 January.

Thursday 13th January 2022

On this day

532

The Nika riots break out in Constantinople as fans of the Blues and Greens chariot teams unite to overthrow Emperor Justinian. The riot is crushed after five days when the Blues withdraw their support upon learning that Justinian also supports their team.

Friday 14th January 2022

On this day

1794

Physician Jesse Bennett performs the first successful Caesarean section on his wife, inside a log cabin in Virginia. The event is only made public after Bennett's death, as he believed he would be mocked as a liar.

Sat 15th & Sun 16th January 2022

On this day

15th January 2009

Captain Chesley Sullenberger guides US Airways Flight 1549 to land in the Hudson River after a birdstrike destroys both engines soon after takeoff. Nicknamed 'The Miracle on the Hudson', it is regarded as the most successful water landing in aviation history.

On this day

1950

Monday 17th January 2022

After two years of planning, a gang of 11 men rob the Brink's Building in Boston, stealing $29.5 million in today's money. Few clues were left and the thieves were caught only after turning on each other, five days before the statute of limitations was due to end.

On this day

1983

Tuesday 18th January 2022

The IOC restores Jim Thorpe's gold medals, 70 years after they were removed for violating the strict amateur rule in place at the 1912 Olympics. Thorpe's trangression was playing baseball for a small sum of money as a young man.

On this day

2001

Wednesday 19th January 2022

Mexican drug lord Joaquin Guzman, known as El Chapo, escapes prison for the first time by bribing his guards and being wheeled out in a laundry cart by accomplices. He remains on the run for 13 years before recapture in 2014

Thursday 20th January 2022

On this day

1945

Franklin D. Roosevelt is sworn in for the fourth time, a remarkable feat which is never to be repeated. Roosevelt's unshakeable popularity leads to the introduction of the 22nd Amendment, which places a two term limit on US presidencies.

Friday 21st January 2022

On this day

2008

Marie Smith Jones, the last native speaker of the Eyak language of Alaska, dies. A Frenchman has since taught himself the language and is now the only fluent speaker, but Eyak is classified as dormant as no native speakers remain alive.

Sat 22nd & Sun 23rd January 2022

On this day

22nd January 1905

Peaceful demonstrators in St Petersburg are fired upon outside the Winter Palace whilst attempting to petition the Tsar. The Revolution of 1905 begins from this event and it is regarded as a precursor to the 1917 Russian Revolution.

On this day

1848

Monday 24th January 2022

James Marshall discovers gold at Sutter's Mill, sparking the California Gold Rush. The population of San Francisco increases from 800 to 100,000 by 1849. Sadly for Marshall, the sawmill he was a partner in fails as all of the employees leave in search of gold.

On this day

1890

Tuesday 25th January 2022

Journalist Nellie Bly completes her solo circumnavigation of the world in 72 days, breaking the 80 day world record of George Francis Train. The expedition had been inspired by Jules Verne's novel *Around the World in Eighty Days*, which had been based on Train.

On this day

1945

Wednesday 26th January 2022

Lt. Audie Murphy of the US Army singlehandedly holds off a German attack in Holtzwihr by climbing a burning tank and manning its machine gun, surviving with only a leg wound. He is later awarded the Medal of Honour for his heroism.

Thursday 27th January 2022

Friday 28th January 2022

Sat 29th & Sun 30th January 2022

Monday 31st January 2022

1943

Field Marshal Friedrich Paulus surrenders to the Soviet Army at Stalingrad, after being denied permission to do so. 107,000 German soldiers are taken into captivity and only 6,000 survive, Paulus among them.

_____

_____

_____

_____

_____

Tuesday 1st February 2022

1887

Having failed to make a success of growing fruit on the land, Harvey Wilcox subdivides the 120 acre ranch he owns in California and sells it as real estate development. It is named Hollywood and later becomes the centre of the US film industry.

_____

_____

_____

_____

_____

Wednesday 2nd February 2022

1709

Alexander Selkirk is rescued after five years spent as a castaway in the South Pacific. He was abandoned by his captain for voicing safety concerns and became adept at surviving using the island's resources. His story inspires the novel *Robinson Crusoe*.

_____

_____

_____

_____

_____

Thursday 3rd February 2022

A low-flying United States Marine Corp plane severs a cable car in Cavalese, Italy, killing 20. The pilots are found guilty of obstruction of justice and dismissed from the Marine Corps, but are acquitted of all criminal charges.

Friday 4th February 2022

As the Maratha army tries to retake Kondhana fort from the Mughals, Tanaji Malusare gets inside by climbing its walls with the help of a trained monitor lizard. He is killed in the ensuing battle, but the fort is won and renamed Sindhagad (Lion's Fort) in his honour.

Sat 5th & Sun 6th February 2022

A plane crash at Munich's airport kills 23, including 8 of Manchester United's most successful team, known as the Busby Babes. The takeoff had been aborted twice, but the captain insisted on trying again rather than fall behind schedule.

Monday 7th February 2022

William Mulcahy breaks a 2,000 year old vase, loaned to the British Museum, while drunk. He is fined £3 and the vase's owner declines to pursue further damages to spare Mulcahy's impoverished family. The vase is now restored and back on display.

Tuesday 8th February 2022

The famously successful racehorse, Shergar, is stolen. A £2 million ransom is initially demanded, but never paid. It has been suggested that the IRA had a hand in the horse's disappearance, but it has never been found and its fate remains a mystery.

Wednesday 9th February 2022

For the second and so far last time in US history, the House of Representatives chooses the President as no candidate in the 1824 election has gained a majority. John Quincy Adams is chosen, despite not winning the popular vote.

Thursday 10th February 2022

1947

Bank robber Willie Sutton escapes prison for the third time by climbing the wall. When searchlights find him, he calls "It's alright!" and is allowed to continue. He stays free for five years, and the man who later turns him in is killed by the American Mafia.

Friday 11th February 2022

On this day

2013

It is announced that Pope Benedict XVI will stand down from the papacy due to ill health. He is only the fifth Pope in history to resign, and the second who was not compelled in some way to stand down, but made the decision himself.

Sat 12th & Sun 13th February 2022

On this day

13th February 1503

Near Barletta, Italy, a drunk French knight disparages the courage of Italians and thus a challenge is made – 13 French vs. 13 Italian knights with the losers agreeing to pay 100 ducats per man. The Italians win and ransom the French as they have brought no money.

Monday 14th February 2022

Souring relations between James Cook's crew and Native Hawaiians comes to a head when Cook attempts to abduct the ruling chief, Kalan'opu'u, to ransom in exchange for a stolen longboat. Cook and four of his men are killed by the Hawaiians.

Tuesday 15th February 2022

Giuseppe Zangara attempts to shoot Franklin D. Roosevelt in Miami, but is forced to stand on a wobbly chair as he is too short to see over the crowd. Perhaps for this reason, his shots go wide and strike five people, killing one, but failing to harm Roosevelt.

Wednesday 16th February 2022

Steven Bradbury becomes the first athlete from the Southern Hemisphere to take a gold medal at a Winter Olympics when he goes from last to first place in the 1,000m speed skating event at Salt Lake City, after all of his opponents fall on the last corner.

Thursday 17th February 2022

On this day

1974

Private Robert K. Preston steals a helicopter, intent on proving his skill as a pilot after failing to complete the Army's helicopter training course. He leads Maryland Police on a one hour chase before being caught on the White House lawn. He receives one year in prison.

Friday 18th February 2022

On this day

1965

Jimmie Lee Jackson is shot and killed during a peaceful march in Marion, Alabama. His death inspires the Selma to Montgomery march led by Martin Luther King, which in turns leads to the Voting Rights Act of 1965.

Sat 19th & Sun 20th February 2022

On this day

19th February 1914

5 year old Charlotte May Pierstorff is sent to her grandparents' house through the post, taking advantage of a 50 pound parcel weight limit. Afterwards the US Postal Service changes its rules to prohibit the shipment of humans.

Monday 21st February 2022

2012

The presidential election in Yemen is held, with Acting President Abd Rabbuh Mansur Hadi as the only candidate on the ballot paper. Despite several boycotts, turnout is good and Hadi is elected president with 100% of the votes.

Tuesday 22nd February 2022

1983

Moose Murders by Arthur Bicknell has its first and only performance on Broadway. Its name has since become shorthand for Broadway failures and it is the standard against which the worst plays are judged.

Wednesday 23rd February 2022

1739

Dick Turpin, using the alias John Palmer and in prison on suspicion of horse stealing, is identified as the infamous highwayman when his old schoolteacher recognises his handwriting in a letter and informs the authorities.

Thursday 24th February 2022

On this day

1942

Reports of an impending Japanese attack lead to a blackout in Los Angeles as anti-aircraft guns comb the skies. It is later found to be a false alarm caused by a weather balloon. Five people die from car accidents or stress-related heart attacks.

Friday 25th February 2022

On this day

1932

Adolf Hitler, an Austrian immigrant, is awarded German citizenship. This allows him to run in the 1932 presidential election. He loses, but is appointed Chancellor by the victor, President Paul von Hindenburg.

Sat 26th & Sun 27th February 2022

On this day

26th February 2013

In Luxor, Egypt, a gas leak causes a fire on a hot air balloon as it attempts to land. Only the pilot and one passenger are able to leap to safety before heat and wind cause the balloon to fly upwards. 18 others die from falling or burns.

Monday 28th February 2022

Roger Scott of Massachusetts is found sleeping in a church and awoken by being smacked in the head with a staff. When he lashes out, he is whipped both for sleeping rough and striking a tithingman, a constable elected to keep order in a church.

Tuesday 1st March 2022

The Battle of Adwa ends the First Italo-Ethiopian War, as a decisive Ethiopian victory destroys Italian aspirations to expand their influence in Africa. Ethiopia is one of only three African countries to remain independent in the 19th century.

Wednesday 2nd March 2022

Rutherford B. Hayes is announced as the winner of the 1876 election, despite not winning the popular vote. Disputes about the electoral vote in four states lead to Democratic concession in exchange for federal troops leaving the South.

Thursday 3th March 2022

1861

Tsar Alexander II signs the Emancipation Manifesto, granting serfs their freedom and full rights as citizens. Many remain bonded to landlords through debts, but it is nevertheless an important step forward in reforming the Russian economy.

Friday 4th March 2022

1933

Three speakers of the Austrian parliament resign, one after another, in a disagreement over a council vote. Chancellor Engelbert Dollfuss uses an emergency decree to form a fascist government, which lasts until the 1938 Anschluss.

Sat 5th & Sun 6th March 2022

5th March 1770

In Boston, British soldiers kill 5 men who are part of a mob throwing snowballs and stones. Of the 8 soldiers involved, only 2 are found guilty of any wrongdoing. The killings heighten anti-British sentiment and are seen as a foundation of the American Revolution.

Thursday 3rd March 2022

1861

Tsar Alexander II signs the Emancipation Manifesto, granting serfs their freedom and full rights as citizens. Many remain bonded to landlords through debts, but it is nevertheless an important step forward in reforming the Russian economy.

Friday 4th March 2022

1933

Three speakers of the Austrian parliament resign, one after another, in a disagreement over a council vote. Chancellor Engelbert Dollfuss uses an emergency decree to form a fascist government, which lasts until the 1938 Anschluss.

Sat 5th & Sun 6th March 2022

5th March 1770

In Boston, British soldiers kill 5 men who are part of a mob throwing snowballs and stones. Of the 8 soldiers involved, only 2 are found guilty of any wrongdoing. The killings heighten anti-British sentiment and are seen as a foundation of the American Revolution.

Thursday 10th March 2022

On this day

1876

Alexander Graham Bell successfully tests his telephone, summoning his assistant Thomas Watson from another room. He proudly records in his journal, "To my delight he came and declared that he had heard and understood what I said."

Friday 11th March 2022

On this day

2010

Sebastián Piñera is sworn in as President of Chile, mere minutes after a 6.9 earthquake strikes further down the coast. The ceremony is concluded quickly and lunch is cancelled to allow the new President to go straight to the disaster zone and get to work.

Sat 12th & Sun 13th March 2022

On this day

13th March 1940

Finland's deadliest sniper, Simo Häyhä, wakes from a coma one week after being shot in the face. The Moscow Peace Treaty is signed on the same day and it is jokingly said that the Soviets fled because they heard he was returning to the fight.

On this day

1757

Admiral John Byng, having failed to keep Minorca out of French hands with undermanned and badly repaired ships, is executed by firing squad. It was quietly believed that he was made a scapegoat by the British government for their loss.

Monday 14th March 2022

On this day

44 BC

Julius Caesar is stabbed to death in the Roman Senate by a conspiracy of 30 men hoping to restore the Roman Republic. The plan fails, as Caesar's death leads to civil war and the ascent of the first Emperor, Caesar's adopted son Augustus.

Tuesday 15th March 2022

On this day

1995

Mississippi becomes the last US state to officially ratify the Thirteenth Amendment which abolishes slavery. All but three states had ratified the amendment between 1865 and 1870. Delaware accepted it in 1901 and Kentucky in 1976.

Wednesday 16th March 2022

Thursday 17th March 2022

1955

Maurice Richard, star player of the Montreal Canadiens ice hockey team, is suspended for assault. A mob of 20,000 fans start a riot which leads to $100,000 in damage alongside arrests and injuries. Richard calls for calm on the radio, successfully cooling tempers.

Friday 18th March 2022

1965

Cosmonaut and Soviet Air Force pilot Alexey Leonov becomes the first man to walk in space, exiting his capsule for 12 minutes. His spacesuit becomes so inflated that he must open a valve and release air in order to get back inside the ship.

Sat 19th & Sun 20th March 2022

20th March 1967

Japanese athlete Shizō Kanakuri completes the marathon of the 1912 Stockholm Olympics, 54 years after he began it. Unable to finish the race, he had left without informing authorities and was regarded as a missing person in Sweden for 50 years.

Monday 21st March 2022

Pope Pius VII is crowned in Venice with a temporary tiara made of papier-mache, as the Papal States had been invaded by the French and his late predecessor removed from Rome, meaning that the Holy See was unavailable.

Tuesday 22nd March 2022

Daredevil Karl Wallenda dies after falling from a high wire in San Juan, Puerto Rico. He was 73 years old. He and his brother Hermann were responsible for creating a three-tier human pyramid which remains unequalled in circus acts today.

Wednesday 23rd March 2022

Waltham Abbey becomes the final monastery to be closed and taken over by King Henry VIII during the Dissolution of the Monasteries, in order to use their income and assets to fund military campaigns.

Thursday 24th March 2022

On this day

1603

James VI of Scotland is named James I of England upon the death of Elizabeth I. James returns to Scotland only once after his accession to the English throne, saying on his way to London that he was "swapping a stony couch for a deep feather bed."

Friday 25th March 2022

On this day

1898

O. Henry is sentenced to five years in prison for embezzlement. While there he begins writing and, from his release in 1902 until his death in 1910, produces more than 600 works. An annual prize for short stories is now named for him.

Sat 26th & Sun 27th March 2022

On this day

26th March 1884

Jurors in Cincinnati return a verdict of manslaughter in a case seen as clear cut murder. Outraged, a mob forms in an attempt to locate and punish both criminal and jurors. Over 4 days, 50 people are killed in one of the most destructive riots in American history.

Monday 28th March 2022

193

Roman Emperor Pertinax is assassinated by his Praetorian guards, who then auction off the Imperial throne. The winner is Didius Julianus, who rules as emperor for nine weeks, after which he is deposed by general Septimius Severus.

Tuesday 29th March 2022

1857

Sepoy Mangal Pandey rebels against the British commanders of the East India Company, attacking Lt. Baugh of the 34th Bengal Native Infantry. His fellow Indians do not stop him, and his actions lead to a series of mutinies that becomes the Indian Rebellion of 1857.

Wednesday 30th March 2022

1928

Amateur jockey William Dutton wins the Grand National astride 100/1 bet Tipperary Tim, after all 41 other horses fall during the race. One other horse, Billy Barton, is re-mounted by the jockey and finishes in second place as the only other horse to complete the race.

Thursday 31st March 2022

A concert in Vienna ends in rioting as the audience are scandalised by the new style of music. Concert organiser Erhard Buschbeck slaps a concertgoer in the face. Composer Oscar Straus later remarks that the slap was the most harmonious sound of the evening.

Friday 1st April 2022

The BBC releases a trailer for *Miracles of Evolution* , a nature film which has discovered flying Adélie penguins. The hoax is so convincing that many viewers expected the full film to be broadcast. It is regarded as one of the best April's Fools hoaxes of the decade.

Sat 2nd & Sun 3rd April 2022

A missing filter at a bio-warfare lab in Sverdlovsk allows the release of anthrax spores, killing approximately 100 people and livestock, although the true death toll is unknown as the incident was covered up by the Soviets and blamed on rotten meat.

Monday 4th April 2022

1841

William Henry Harrison dies after 31 days as US President, becoming the first incumbent to die in office and the shortest-serving in history. His death is blamed on his inauguration 3 weeks before, when he gave a two hour speech in cold and wet weather without a coat.

Tuesday 5th April 2022

1943

Poon Lim, the Chinese steward and only survivor of the torpedoed British ship *SS Benlomond*, is found by fishermen on the coast of Brazil after 133 days of floating on a raft. His survival techniques have since been included in Royal Navy manuals.

Wednesday 6th April 2022

1896

The first modern Olympic Games, revived by Pierre de Coubertin 1,500 years after they were banned in 393 AD, begin in Athens. The Games are a great success and are held every four years since, being cancelled only 3 times during the 20th century.

Thursday 7th April 2022

The crew of Fed-Ex Flight 705 subdue a flight engineer turned suicidal hijacker, via aerial maneouvres and hand-to-hand combat. The 3-man crew are rendered medically unfit to fly again by their injuries, but their heroism saves the plane and all of their lives.

Friday 8th April 2022

The Venus de Milo is found in ruins on the island of Milos, Greece. The statue is later made famous by the Louvre's campaign to make it seem even more desirable than the pieces lost when other countries reclaim their art from Napoleon's collection.

Sat 9th & Sun 10th April 2022

Tombs containing a collection of writings, including chapters of Sun Tzu's *The Art of War* and a presumed lost copy of Sun Bin's *Art of War* are discovered by construction workers in Shandong, China. They are now housed in a specially built museum.

On this day

1993

450 prisoners of 3 usually opposing gang affiliations join forces in Lucasville, Ohio to protest poor conditions and mandatory tuberculosis vaccines. The ensuing riot lasts for 10 days and results in the deaths of 5 inmates and 1 prison guard.

Monday 11th April 2022

On this day

2009

Captain Richard Phillips is rescued by the US Navy five days after being taken hostage in a lifeboat by Somali pirates, three of whom are killed and one captured. The story is made into a film starring Tom Hanks in 2013.

Tuesday 12th April 2022

On this day

1883

Nine years after fleeing the law, Alferd Packer is convicted of murdering his five companions during an expedition in the San Juan Mountains of Colorado in 1874. Upon retrial the charge is reduced to manslaughter and he serves 18 years in prison.

Wednesday 13th April 2022

Thursday 14th April 2022

1865

As Abraham Lincoln is assassinated in Ford's Theatre, US Secretary of State William Seward is attacked in his home. Lewis Powell manages to gain entry to Seward's bedroom, but a metal splint on his jaw protects Seward from being stabbed to death.

Friday 15th April 2022

1955

The first restaurant of the McDonald's franchise is opened by Roy Kroc in Des Plaines, Iowa. The original restaurant was a hamburger stand in San Bernardino, California, owned by two brothers who were chased out by Kroc's ambitious vision.

Sat 16th & Sun 17th April 2022

17th April 1876

Six Irish prisoners who had escaped from the penal colony of Western Australia two days prior are found aboard a ship, but the captain hoists the US flag and warns that any attack would be an act of war. The prisoners are let go to avoid an international incident.

Monday 18th April 2022

High standards for what is deemed 'newsworthy' and a limited ability to independently collect news leads to the 8.45pm BBC News bulletin simply reporting "there is no news" followed by 15 minutes of music.

Tuesday 19th April 2022

Holy Roman Emperor Charles VI, with no male heirs, issues the Pragmatic Sanction of 1713 to ensure that his lands can be inherited by a female. His daughter Maria Theresa becomes the only female ruler of the Holy Roman Empire in 1740.

Wednesday 20th April 2022

Abraham Thornton, rearrested for the murder of Mary Ashford, demands a trial by battle. The court grants his request, but the victim's brother refuses the challenge, and so he is freed. The option for trial by battle is removed from English law in 1819.

Thursday 21st April 2022

The city of Flint, Michigan, changes its water supply from treated water from Lake Huron to the Detroit River, sparking a crisis in which 12,000 people suffer lead poisoning and 15 die from Legionnaire's disease. Two officials are charged with involuntary manslaughter.

Friday 22nd April 2022

At noon, 50,000 people rush into central Oklahoma in order to claim a homestead amongst 2 million acres of 'free' land in the Indian Territory. By the end of the day, Oklahoma City and Guthrie have become established cities of 10,000 people each.

Sat 23rd & Sun 24th April 2022

Duke Wilhelm IV of Bavaria signs the 'German Beer Purity Law' (Reinheitsgebot) which decrees that beer in Germany can only be made from three ingredients – water, malt and hops – ensuring a common standard throughout the country.

On this day

1962

Monday 25th April 2022

Baseball player Harry Chiti is traded to the New York Mets in exchange for an unnamed player. On 15 June, the Mets return him to his original Cleveland team, making him the first American baseball player to be traded for himself.

On this day

1478

Tuesday 26th April 2022

The noble Pazzi family of Florence attack Lorenzo and Giuliano de'Medici during Mass, intending to overthrow the Medicis. Lorenzo survives and the family are banned from the city, with everything bearing their name and coat of arms erased.

On this day

1667

Wednesday 27th April 2022

John Milton sells his epic poem, *Paradise Lost*, to a printer for £10. The ten books, telling the story of Adam and Eve, is now regarded as Milton's magnum opus and the work which earned his reputation as one of England's best contemporary poets.

Thursday 28th April 2022

On this day

1789

Captain Bligh and 18 men are set adrift in the Pacific Ocean following a mutiny on *HMS Bounty*. The men survive the ordeal to reach land on 14 June, although six later succumb to illness. Only one mutineer escapes death or punishment.

Friday 29th April 2022

On this day

1975

The US evacuates its citizens from Saigon as the North Vietnamese forces advance. Helicopters are used as airport runways are too damaged. Code-named Operation Frequent Wind, the evacuation marks the end of US involvement in Vietnam.

Sat 30th & Sun 1st May 2022

On this day

30th April 1900

Locomotive engineer Casey Jones is killed when his passenger train collides with a freight train. He orders the fireman to jump out and manages to lower the speed of the train from 75mph to 35mph in 91 metres, making himself the only fatality.

Monday 2nd May 2022

While returning to camp following the Battle of Chancellorsville, Stonewall Jackson and his men are mistaken for the enemy and hit by friendly fire. Jackson dies 8 days later, remarking that "I have always wished to die on a Sunday."

Tuesday 3rd May 2022

Britain's only General Strike begins. 1.75 million people stop work to show support to striking miners, but volunteers keep the country running and union leaders are forced to halt the action after 10 days. A law banning sympathetic strike action is passed in 1927

Wednesday 4th May 2022

A peaceful protest for an eight hour work day in Haymarket Square, Chicago, goes awry when a bomb is thrown at police and the crowd is fired on. International Workers' Day, also known as Labour Day in the USA or May Day in the UK, is created by this event.

Thursday 5th May 2022

1945

German forces led by Josef Gangl and American forces led by John Lee work together to protect Castle Itter in Austria from an SS attack, and save the French prisoners inside. It is the only known occasion during WWII when enemy forces fight together.

Friday 6th May 2022

1937

At Lakehurst, New Jersey, the German airship Hindenburg bursts into flames whilst attempting to land. Public confidence in airship safety never recovers and the disaster marks the sudden end of a travel industry that until then had looked promising.

Sat 7th & Sun 8th May 2022

8th May 1984

Denis Lortie kills 3 and wounds 13 at the Parliament Building in Quebec. A higher death toll is prevented as René Jalbert approaches the gunman, persuading him to let people leave and making himself a hostage for four hours until Lortie surrenders to police.

On this day

1671

Thomas Blood attempts to steal the Crown Jewels, but is caught before escaping the Tower of London. King Charles II, supposed to have a certain respect for boldness, pardons Blood and awards him land in Ireland worth £500 per year.

Monday 9th May 2022

On this day

1849

Tensions between working-class and wealthy theatregoers boil over at the Astor Opera House in New York. A dispute between actors Edwin Forrest and William Macready cause a riot between their fans and serve to further cement the class segregation of theatre.

Tuesday 10th May 2022

On this day

1812

Spencer Perceval is shot in the lobby of the House of Commons, the only British Prime Minister ever to be assassinated. His killer, John Bellingham, had been refused compensation by the British government for false imprisonment in Russia.

Wednesday 11th May 2022

Thursday 12th May 2022

While on a pilgrimage of thanks for his life being spared in an assassination attempt almost exactly one year prior, Pope John Paul II is once again attacked, this time by a Catholic priest in Fátima, Portugal. The Pope is uninjured and blesses the attacker.

Friday 13th May 2022

Slave Robert Smalls takes over *CSS Planter* and sails towards the Union lines, freeing himself and all of the enslaved crew aboard. The ship becomes a Union warship and Smalls is appointed captain. He becomes a politican after the Civil War.

Sat 14th & Sun 15th May 2022

Spanish inventor Diego Marín Aquilera attempts one of the first manned flights in a glider. He intends to soar to a nearby town, but instead flies for 300-400 metres before crash-landing, never reaching more than 5 or 6 metres off the ground.

Monday 16th May 2022

Andrew Johnson evades impeachment by one vote. A precedent is thus set for the president's ability to disagree with Congress without being removed, which ultimately assists in maintaining checks and balances as it prevents partisan action.

Tuesday 17th May 2022

Pánfilo de Narváez leads 600 people on an expedition to form colonial settlements on the Gulf Coast. Within a year, all but 80 are lost or killed. These 80 spend the next 8 years travelling on foot to reach Mexico City, and only 4 arrive safely.

Wednesday 18th May 2022

Mount St. Helen's erupts in Washington, killing 57 people. Scientists are taken off guard as the volcano erupts through a bulge on its side, rather than the expected upward trajectory, with the result that safe zones were drawn incorrectly.

Thursday 19th May 2022

Friday 20th May 2022

Sat 21st & Sun 22nd May 2022

On this day

1618

The Thirty Years War is sparked when two Catholic lords and a secretary are thrown from a window in Prague. They survive the fall, claiming the Virgin Mary interceded to help them, while the Protestants suggest it was because they landed on a dung heap.

Monday 23rd May 2022

On this day

1567

King Erik XIV of Sweden, in a fit of madness, orders the deaths of five noble prisoners and his tutor. His guards are ordered to spare "Herr Sten" and two prisoners of that name survive as the guards weren't sure which was being referred to.

Tuesday 24th May 2022

On this day

1935

Jesse Owens, at the time attending Ohio State University, breaks three world records and equals a fourth during the Big Ten Conference track and field meeting in Ann Arbor, Michigan. It has been called "the greatest 45 minutes ever in sport."

Wednesday 25th May 2022

Thursday 26th May 2022

Action Park opens in New Jersey, swiftly gaining a reputation for its poorly designed and unsafe amusements. It sees 6 deaths and countless serious injuries until its closure in 1996, but is recalled fondly by those who grew up during its zenith.

Friday 27th May 2022

The Islamist group Abu Sayyaf take 20 hostages at a tourist resort on the island of Palawan in the Philippines. Over the next year, approximately 100 hostages are taken and 20 murdered, until the last one is recovered on 7 June 2002.

Sat 28th & Sun 29th May 2022

18 year old German Mathias Rust lands a rented plane in Red Square, having avoided what was supposed to be an impenetrable security system. The reputation of the Soviet military suffers greatly and many senior officers lose their jobs as a result.

On this day

Monday 30th May 2022

1896

New York's first traffic collision occurs as Henry Wells strikes cyclist Ebeling Thomas on Broadway, fracturing his leg. On the same day, seven cyclists are arrested for speeding. The judge scolds, "Some of you people think no-one has a right in the street but yourselves."

On this day

Tuesday 31st May 2022

1669

Samuel Pepys writes the last entry in his famous diary. Spanning a decade, the diary provides eyewitness testimony of numerous prominent events in the 1660s and is one of the most important documents of the English Restoration.

On this day

Wednesday 1st June 2022

1773

In South Africa, dairy farmer Wolraad Woltemade rides his horse into the sea in order to rescue sailors from the sinking ship *De Jonge Thomas*. He successfully rescues 14 men, but he and his exhausted horse sadly drown on their eighth attempt to swim out.

Thursday 2nd June 2022

Chile and Italy meet at the 1962 World Cup in a match known as the Battle of Santiago, due to the level of violence exhibited. Two players are sent off and police intervention is required on four occasions. Chile wins by two goals to zero.

Friday 3rd June 2022

The Zoot Suit Riots in Los Angeles begin, as an altercation between sailors and Mexican-American youths devolves into a city-wide mob of servicemen and civilians attacking and stripping anyone they perceive to be Latino, regardless of age or gender.

Sat 4th & Sun 5th June 2022

A lone man blocks a column of tanks at Tiananmen Square, Beiijing, using only his body and two shopping bags. He is able to stop the tanks twice before being removed. His identity and fate are unknown, but his image remains a powerful symbol of resistance.

Monday 6th June 2022

Boatman Alexis St. Martin is shot and survives with a hole in his stomach. Doctor William Beaumont seizes the chance to further his studies into digestion and his experiments lead to 51 new discoveries, although St. Martin eventually abandons him in 1834.

Tuesday 7th June 2022

In the second Sino-Japanese war, the Chinese government flood the Yellow River to halt the Japanese advance. However this kills 800,000, makes swathes of farmland unusuable and turns several districts into guerilla bases as people turn against both sides.

Wednesday 8th June 2022

Submarine *USS Barbaro* delivers the only example of missile mail, firing a cruise missile with mail containers in place of a warhead towards the naval station in Florida. The mail arrives safely, but it is decided that the cost of missile mail could never be justified.

Thursday 9th June 2022

On this day

1935

Alcoholic doctor Bob Smith drinks a beer after suffering tremors due to withdrawal. The next day he and fellow alcoholic Bill Wilson create a support group that becomes known as Alcoholics Anonymous. Smith remains sober for the rest of his life.

Friday 10th June 2022

On this day

1990

Captain Timothy Lancaster is pulled out of the cockpit and pinned to the fuselage of BA Flight 5390 when a badly installed window panel comes loose. He is trapped outside for 20 minutes as the plane makes an emergency landing, but miraculously survives.

Sat 11th & Sun 12th June 2022

On this day

11th June 1928

Morris Frank demonstrates the abilities of his new Swiss guide dog, Buddy, on busy roads in New York City. Buddy is the first guide dog assigned to a blind US citizen, and Frank goes on to found the first guide dog training school in the USA.

On this day

1881

The naval exploration ship *USS Jeanette* is crushed by ice on the Siberian coast, forcing its crew to abandon it as it sinks. The two lifeboats of men are separated, with 13 men finding rescue in a native village while another 12 are lost.

Monday 13th June 2022

On this day

2017

A left wing activist opens fire on Republican Congressmen practicing for a charity baseball game, injuring five. The baseball game happens the next day, raising $1 million for charity. The Democrats win decisively, but loan the trophy to the Republicans.

Tuesday 14th June 2022

On this day

1985

Rembrandt's painting *Danaë* is vandalised with a knife and sulphuric acid by Bronius Maigys, who was later judged to be insane, at the Hermitage Museum in St Petersburg. Restoration on the painting was completed in 1997.

Wednesday 15th June 2022

Thursday 16th June 2022

Dancer Rudolf Nureyev defects from the Soviet Union during a tour with the Kirov Ballet, when he becomes suspicious of orders to return to the Soviet Union rather than continue the tour to London. He escapes his KGB minders and is given asylum in France.

Friday 17th June 2022

Mumtaz Mahal, Empress of the Mughal Empire, dies in childbirth. Her husband Shah Jahan is inconsolable and spends the next 22 years planning and building a grand mausoleum for her, the Taj Mahal. Mumtaz and Shah Jahan are both buried there.

Sat 18th & Sun 19th June 2022

Charles Darwin receives an essay by Alfred Russel which reveals that Russel had independently created a theory of evolution. Darwin swiftly publishes the essay alongside his own writing, which had been awaiting publication for 20 years.

Monday 20th June 2022

Kazimierz Piechowski and three other prisoners steal SS uniforms and a staff car, and drive through the front gates of Auschwitz to freedom. Three of the four are never recaptured. The practice of tattooing inmates is created to prevent another such escape.

Tuesday 21st June 2022

The USA bloodlessly captures the island of Guam from Spain. The Spanish were unaware that they were at war and thought the shots from the US ship were a friendly salute. Upon climbing aboard to welcome the visitors, they were taken as prisoners of war.

Wednesday 22nd June 2022

The trial of Erasmus Shue for the murder of Elva Zona Heaster begins. According to legend, his conviction is partly based on the testimony of the victim's mother, who claimed that her daughter's ghost named Shue as the killer.

Thursday 23rd June 2022

Friday 24th June 2022

Sat 25th & Sun 26th June 2022

1844

Monday 27th June 2022

Joseph and Hyrum Smith are killed by a mob in Carthage Jail in Illinois. The Latter Day Saints thus suffer a succession crisis and splinter into three groups, with most moving to the Utah Territory and continuing as the Mormon church that is best-known today.

1880

Tuesday 28th June 2022

Australian bushranger and murderer Ned Kelly is captured following a shootout with police, while wearing a suit of homemade armour to repel bullets. He is defeated when a policeman notices that the armour does not cover his legs and brings him to the ground.

1971

Wednesday 29th June 2022

The three-man Soviet crew of *Soyuz 11* are found dead inside their capsule upon returning from the *Salyut 1* space station. It is found that they suffocated when a pressurisation valve failed. The Sokol space suit was invented as a result and is still used today.

Thursday 30th June 2022

Friday 1st July 2022

Sat 2nd & Sun 3rd July 2022

Monday 4th July 2022

During a picnic, 10 year old Alice Liddell asks her family's friend Charles Dodgson (an author under the pen name of Lewis Carroll) to tell her a story. The tale he creates is later written down and published as *Alice's Adventures in Wonderland* .

Tuesday 5th July 2022

Unable to find a model for his risque creation, designer Louis Réard hires 18 year old nude dancer Micheline Bernardini to showcase his two-piece swimsuit, named a bikini, at a public pool in Paris. The design is a huge hit and Bernardini receives 50,000 fan letters.

Wednesday 6th July 2022

The Spartans lose to the Thebans at the Battle of Leuctra, stripping them of their power and prestige. The future Alexander the Great, son of the Macedonian king, later employs Theban tactics to conquer great swathes of land across the world.

Thursday 7th July 2022

The first loaf of sliced bread is sold by the Chillcothe Baking Company in Missouri, coincidentally on the 48th birthday of Otto Frederick Rohwedder, who had invented the machine which both sliced and wrapped the bread for sale.

Friday 8th July 2022

The first four boys of a junior football team in Thailand are rescued from the Tham Luang Nang Non caves, where they had been trapped by heavy rain since 23 June. Over the next two days, the remaining 8 boys and their coach are rescued.

Sat 9th & Sun 10th July 2022

Daniel Hale Williams performs the first successful heart surgery at Provident Hospital in Chicago, the USA's first non-segregated hospital which he had founded, without anaesthetic or blood transfusion. His patient survives and lives for 20 years.

Monday 11th July 2022

The Mexican drug lord known as El Chapo escapes from prison for the second time by digging a tunnel under his cell. It is fitted with lights, air ducts and even a motorcycle to carry him to freedom. He is recaptured in January 2016 after a shootout.

Tuesday 12th July 2022

1,300 striking miners are abducted from Bisbee, Arizona by vigilantes. They are moved for 16 hours on manure-lined trains without food or water, and abandoned in the New Mexico desert. The action is condemned as illegal, but no-one is prosecuted.

Wednesday 13th July 2022

Lightning strikes cause a citywide blackout in New York. The night is marked by high levels of crime, particularly looting and arson, which have since been attributed to a financial crisis, paranoia over recent serial killer activity and a summer heatwave.

Thursday 14th July 2022

On this day

1865

Edward Whymper and his party become the first to ascend the Matterhorn. One of the party slips while descending, with the rope attaching the climbers dragging four others after him. A weak point causes the rope to snap, saving Whymper and two others.

Friday 15th July 2022

On this day

1875

"Rainmaker" Charles Hatfield is born. He was famously hired by San Diego city council to fill the Morena Dam reservoir in 1915, with the resulting downpour causing destructive flooding. Hatfield was cleared of causing the damage, but denied his fee.

Sat 16th & Sun 17th July 2022

On this day

17th July 1938

Douglas Corrigan flies 'the wrong way', misreading his compass and taking his plane from New York to Ireland rather than to California as intended. He had been denied permission to fly to Ireland, and never admitted whether his 'mistake' was intentional.

Monday 18th July 2022

The Ballot Act introduces secret ballots for UK elections, allowing tenants to vote against the wishes of their landlords and retailers against the wishes of their customers for the first time. The first ballot box is used for a by-election on 15 August.

Tuesday 19th July 2022

Italian judge Paolo Borsellino and five others are killed by a Mafia car bomb, 57 days after his friend and fellow judge Giovanni Falcone was murdered in the same way. A notebook Borsellino used to write about his investigations has never been found.

Wednesday 20th July 2022

Patrick Sawyer collapses in an airport in Nigeria after arriving from Liberia, dying of Ebola on 24 July. 19 cases and 8 deaths are traced to his arrival, but health workers in Lagos are able to prevent an epidemic. Nigeria is declared Ebola-free on 20 October 2014.

Thursday 21st July 2022

Friday 22nd July 2022

Sat 23rd & Sun 24th July 2022

Monday 25th July 2022

The English ship *Sea Venture* is driven ashore on modern-day Bermuda to avoid being sunk in a storm while sailing to Virginia. The colonists aboard are stranded for nine months. The story is said to have inspired William Shakespeare's play *The Tempest*.

Tuesday 26th July 2022

Samir Geagea, convicted of political assassinations in 1994, is granted amnesty by the newly elected Lebanese Parliament and released after 11 years of solitary confinement inside a windowless cell beneath the Ministry of Defence building.

Wednesday 27th July 2022

Dutch artist Vincent van Gogh shoots himself in the chest, dying two days later. Unsuccessful in his lifetime, he is romanticised as the archetype of a tortured artist and his paintings are now among the most expensive to have ever been sold.

Thursday 28th July 2022

On this day

1866

Vinnie Ream becomes the youngest and first female artist to receive a commission from the US government. At 18 years old, her bust of Abraham Lincoln is chosen to be made into a full-size statue, which is unveiled in 1871 and still stands in the Capitol Rotunda.

Friday 29th July 2022

On this day

1907

Robert Baden-Powell creates the week-long Brownsea Island Sports Camp on the south coast of England, bringing boys of different social classes together for outdoor activities. The event is regarded as the founding of the now international Scout Movement.

Sat 30th & Sun 31st July 2022

On this day

30th July 1943

Australian stretcher bearer Corporal Leslie "Bull" Allen saves the lives of 12 wounded American soldiers at Mount Tambu in New Guinea, carrying them one by one on his back whilst under fire from the Japanese. He is awarded the US Silver Star for his bravery.

Monday 1st August 2022

Chilean Navy ship *Joven Daniel* is reported as wrecked near Araucanía. Inability to discover the fate of its passengers and stories of murder by the native Mapuche tribe contributes to Chile's later decision to invade the previously independent tribal lands.

Tuesday 2nd August 2022

Olivier de Clisson is executed on suspicion of treason. His wife Jeanne swears revenge and sells her family estates, raising an army and warships to begin a life of piracy against the French. She continues for 13 years before marrying again and resuming a normal life.

Wednesday 3rd August 2022

One of the world's deadliest wildfires kills 1,200 people at the Kursha-2 settlement in the Soviet Union. The majority of deaths occur aboard a train sent to evacuate the residents, which was trapped by a burning bridge. Only 20 people escape.

Thursday 4th August 2022

On this day

1693

Today is the date traditionally ascribed to Dom Pérignon's invention of champagne. It is not clear if he actually invented champagne, which became a popular drink only in the 19th century, but he undoubtedly pioneered new methods for the creation of sparkling wine.

Friday 5th August 2022

On this day

2010

A cave in at the San Jose copper-gold mine in Chile traps thirty-three men underground. An international effort is launched to rescue them and all of the miners are recovered, alive and with no long-term injuries, on 13 October 2010.

Sat 6th & Sun 7th August 2022

On this day

6th August 1915

German troops fire poison gas on a garrison of Russian soldiers at Osowiec Fortress in Poland, expecting to meet no resistance as they advance. To their horror, 100 Russians charge them and the Germans, terrified at the sight of 'dead men' fighting, retreat.

Monday 8th August 2022

A fight between a drunken man and a thirteen year old girl on the street outside National League Park in Philadelphia causes a curious crowd to gather on a balcony. The platform comes loose from its supports and falls 30m, killing 12 and injuring 232.

Tuesday 9th August 2022

Singapore becomes the only sovereign nation to be made independent unwillingly, when social unrest and political tension leads the Parliament of Malaysia to make a unilateral decision to expel them, a mere two years after the countries merged.

Wednesday 10th August 2022

The Swedish warship *Vasa* sinks 20 minutes into her maiden voyage. Despite the efforts of a committee to find a scapegoat, no-one is ultimately punished and the disaster is blamed on shipbuilder Henrik Hybertsson, who had died a year prior to the launch.

Thursday 11th August 2022

During sound check for a weekly radio address, Ronald Reagan jokes that "I've signed legislation that will outlaw Russia forever. We begin bombing in five minutes." The remark is not broadcast live, but is later leaked and causes a brief alert in the Soviet Union.

Friday 12th August 2022

Joseph Lister, inspired by the work of Louis Pasteur and experimenting with carbolic acid to prevent micro-organisms entering wounds, successfully performs the world's first antiseptic surgery on a seven year old boy at Glasgow Royal Infirmary.

Sat 13th & Sun 14th August 2022

Two young women camping at Glacier National Park in Montana are killed by bears in separate incidents, the first attacks in the park's 57 year history. The 'Night of the Grizzlies' leads to an overhaul in previously lax national park safety throughout the USA.

Monday 15th August 2022

19 year old border guard Konrad Schumann leaps over the Berlin Wall, at the time only a single line of barbed wire, after protestors lead him to reconsider which side he wants to be on. He remains in West Germany for the rest of his life.

Tuesday 16th August 2022

The Dole Air Race from California to Hawaii begins, inspired by Charles Lindbergh's successful trans-Atlantic flight. Only 8 planes of the original 15 take off, and of these only 2 make it to Hawaii. The other 6 crash in the ocean or are damaged beyond repair.

Wednesday 17th August 2022

44 year old Bridget Driscoll is the first pedestrian to be killed by a motor vehicle. She is struck by a car travelling at 4mph in London. The jury returned a verdict of accidental death and the coroner added that he hoped "such a thing would never happen again."

Thursday 18th August 2022

Governor of the Roanoke colony, John White, returns from a supply trip to England to find the colony abandoned. The word 'Croatoan', referring to a nearby tribe, is carved into a fence, but no other evidence of the colony's fate has ever been found.

Friday 19th August 2022

The doors of Cinema Rex in Abadan, Iran are locked and the building set on fire. Approximately 420 people die. The event is regarded as a major provocation for the 1979 Revolution which overthrew the Shah, whom many people believed to be responsible.

Sat 20th & Sun 21st August 2022

An F5 tornado strikes Southeast Minnesota. At the time the city of Rochester had no medical facilities nearby to treat the injured. A local doctor, William Mayo, subsequently creates the Mayo Clinic which has since been listed as one of the best hospitals in the United States.

Monday 22nd August 2022

Two paintings by Edvard Munch, a version of *The Scream* and *Madonna*, are stolen at gunpoint from the Munch Museum in Oslo. The paintings are recovered safely on 31 August 2006 and three men are convicted of the theft.

Tuesday 23rd August 2022

Four people are taken hostage in Kreditbanken in Stockholm during a failed robbery. Over the following five days, the hostages come to trust their captor more than the police, a phenomenon that becomes known as Stockholm syndrome.

Wednesday 24th August 2022

The suspension of payments in a New York bank brings public attention to a stock market decline and sparks a panic. Thanks to the recent invention of the telegraph, this is the first financial crisis to spread throughout the USA and worldwide.

Thursday 25th August 2022

Friday 26th August 2022

Sat 27th & Sun 28th August 2022

Monday 29th August 2022

The Incan emperor, Atahualpa, is killed by the Spanish even after a ransom is paid for his safe return. The Incan empire collapses after his death and the Spanish install their own puppet emperor, completing their conquest of the Inca people.

Tuesday 30th August 2022

The crew of Ernest Shackleton's ship *Endurance*, who have been trapped on Elephant Island for four months, are finally rescued. Shackleton and five others had sailed 720 miles in a lifeboat and walked a further 32 miles to reach help at a whaling station.

Wednesday 31st August 2022

The first in a series of Russian bombings occurs in a Moscow shopping mall. Five further bombings, blamed on Chechen extremists, occur through September and contribute to both the Second Chechen War and Vladimir Putin's ascension to the presidency.

Thursday 1st September 2022

On this day

1173

Four months into the siege of Ancona by Imperial forces, a woman known as Stamira sacrifices herself to destroy enemy weapons, giving Ancona time to restore food supplies. This allows the city to hold out until reinforcements arrive in October.

Friday 2nd September 2022

On this day

31 BC

Octavian attains victory at the Battle of Actium as Cleopatra's fleet retreats, soon followed by Mark Antony's. Mark Antony's army then abandon him. It is noted as the end of the Roman Republic as Octavian becomes the first Emperor in 27 BC.

Sat 3rd & Sun 4th September 2022

On this day

3rd September 301

Saint Marinus is said to have become a hermit on Monte Titano and begun to build a monastery on this date. His reputation for piety enticed others to follow him there and this community grew into San Marino, the world's oldest republic.

Monday 5th September 2022

Pan Am 73 is hijacked on the ground in Karachi, but the crew escape thanks to the warning of 23 year old Neerja Bhanot, who also hides the passports of American passengers. She and 43 others do not survive, but Bhanot is later given India's highest award for bravery.

Tuesday 6th September 2022

US President William McKinley is assassinated by an anarchist at a World Fair in Buffalo, having refused security as he enjoyed meeting the public. His death leads to legislation which gives the Secret Service full-time responsibility for presidential protection.

Wednesday 7th September 2022

Pirate Henry Every commits the most profitable raid in history until that point, capturing £600,000 worth of gold and jewels from Mughal Empire ships. This raid led to the first worldwide manhunt, but Every was never found and no records of him exist after 1696.

Thursday 8th September 2022

Vietnam veteran Leonard Matlovich appears in uniform on the cover of *Time*, outing himself as homosexual in hopes of challenging the US Army's ban on gay servicemen. He is discharged, but continues to work as an activist until his death in 1988.

Friday 9th September 2022

The first instance of a computer bug is noted by Grace Hopper, a scientist working on the programming of the Harvard Mark II computer, when she finds a moth inside the relays. The term 'bug' is still used to refer to any external disruption to computer operations.

Sat 10th & Sun 11th September 2022

A group of thieves break into the Royal Storehouse and steal France's Crown Jewels. Most are later recovered, but the 67 carat French Blue is never seen again. It is believed to have been cut into two pieces, with the larger becoming known as the Hope Diamond.

Monday 12th September 2022

French ships rescue 4,000 Armenians, the population of six villages, from the mountain of Musa Dagh in Turkey. The people had been trapped for 53 days, resisting Ottoman attempts to deport them, and had just run out of supplies when they were found.

Tuesday 13th September 2022

Railroad worker Phineas Gage is impaled through the head with an iron bar, miraculously surviving with no loss of function, but with severe changes to his character. The case is the first indicator of brain damage's effect on personality.

Wednesday 14th September 2022

Amateur poet Francis Scott Key is inspired by an American flag waving above Fort McHenry, following the US victory in the Battle of Baltimore, and writes a poem which is later set to music and becomes the US national anthem, *The Star-Spangled Banner*.

Thursday 15th September 2022

Friday 16th September 2022

Sat 17th & Sun 18th September 2022

Monday 19th September 2022

The Electoral Act makes New Zealand the first country to allow votes for women. Australia follows suit in 1894 whilst also allowing women to stand for election, and Finland becomes the third in 1906, also providing those benefits to indigenous people.

Tuesday 20th September 2022

An 8.6 magnitude earthquake off the coast of Japan triggers a tsunami. Alongside other damage, the water completely destroys the building which houses the Great Buddha statue at Kōtoku-in monastery. The statue itself is undamaged and has sat outside ever since.

Wednesday 21st September 2022

North Korean pilot No Kum-sok defects, flying his aircraft to a South Korean air force base and landing the wrong way, which saved him from being seen and shot down. To his surprise, he is given a $100,000 reward for defecting with a working aircraft.

Thursday 22nd September 2022

On this day

1892

At the village of Lindal-in-Furness, No. 115 locomotive is swallowed by a sinkhole so large that the train disappears from view. Fortunately only two people were aboard and both jumped clear in time. The story has since inspired several stories and even a TV show.

Friday 23rd September 2022

On this day

1780

British Major John André is arrested by the US Army and intelligence found on his person implicates high-ranking US general Benedict Arnold as a traitor. Washington's trust in Arnold leads to a slow reaction, however, and gives Arnold time to escape to the British.

Sat 24th & Sun 25th September 2022

On this day

24th September 1929

James Doolittle completes a flight in a windowless plane, relying entirely on cockpit instruments and opening the possibility of all-weather flying. He later invents the artificial horizon and heading indicator, which are ubiquitous in a modern cockpit.

Monday 26th September 2022

A radar signal warning of five missiles launched from the USA is judged a false alarm by Stanislav Petrov, who is suspicious of how few missiles have been launched. The radar is later found to be faulty and Petrov credited with avoiding a possible nuclear war.

Tuesday 27th September 2022

Urban VII dies of malaria only 13 days after being elected Pope, making his papacy the shortest in history. He makes use of his brief time to create the world's first smoking ban, threatening excommunication to any who used tobacco in or around a church.

Wednesday 28th September 2022

Alexander Fleming returns to his laboratory after a month long holiday to discover a mould has grown on one of his culture plates, destroying the staphylococci bacteria he was studying. The mould, named Penicillium, becomes the base for the antibiotic penicillin.

Thursday 29th September 2022

Two Australian Air Force Avro Anson planes collide in mid-air during a training exercise, becoming attached to each other. The pilot of the upper plane discovers he can control the two aircraft and makes a safe emergency landing, with all four crew surviving.

Friday 30th September 2022

Serbian soldier Radoje Ljutovac becomes the first in history to shoot down an aircraft from the ground. In recognition of this achievement, he receives a horse, military decoration and promotion. After the war he opens a mixed goods store.

Sat 1st & Sun 2nd October 2022

In Syracuse, a group of abolitionists break into a courtroom to free William Henry, an escaped slave known as Jerry. He is hidden in the home of a well-known anti-abolitionist for four days before being transported to Canada, where he settled.

Monday 3rd October 2022

The shooting down of a Black Hawk helicopter over Mogadishu causes the deaths of 19 US soldiers and numerous Somali casualities. The public outcry is credited as one reason why the USA refused to offer assistance during the Rwandan genocide six months later.

Tuesday 4th October 2022

Austrian F1 driver Jochen Rindt becomes the only posthumous winner of the Drivers' Championship when Jacky Ickx finishes 4th at US Grand Prix. Rindt died at the Italian Grand Prix on 5 September, having won five races, and no driver was able to match his lead.

Wednesday 5th October 2022

A national recall of Tylenol is ordered in the USA following seven deaths in Chicago attributed to cyanide poisoning. The tampering leads to the introduction of security bands on bottles and the replacement of capsule tablets with solid caplets.

Thursday 6th October 2022

On this day

1985

PC Keith Blakelock is killed during riots at the Broadwater Farm estate in London, when he trips during a police retreat and is attacked by 50 people. The case has been investigated four times and seven people charged, but no-one has ever been convicted of his murder.

Friday 7th October 2022

On this day

1916

An American football game between Georgia Tech Engineers and Cumberland College Bulldogs leads to the most lopsided score in the history of college football, as Georgia Tech attain victory with a score of 222-0.

Sat 8th & Sun 9th October 2022

On this day

8th October 1480

The Great Stand on the Ugra River begins. After four days of fighting, the forces of Ivan II and Akhmat Khan realise not even their arrows can cross the wide river and begin a month long standoff, which ends on 26 October as Ivan withdraws his army ahead of the winter.

Monday 10th October 2022

A Boeing 247 becomes the first proven case of sabotage on a commercial aircraft when an explosive device in the rear baggage compartment detonates. All 7 people aboard are discounted as suspects and the saboteur's identity remains unknown.

Tuesday 11th October 2022

Anita Hill testifies that Clarence Thomas, about to be elected to the Supreme Court, sexually harassed her ten years prior. Her testimony does not prevent his election, but is seen as a contributing factor to the large numbers of women elected to Congress in 1992.

Wednesday 12th October 2022

Prince Ludwig marries Princess Therese. Over the next few days, a festival is thrown for the citizens of Munich to join the celebrations, including horse races, a costume parade and singing. The spectacle is repeated in 1811 and becomes the annual Oktoberfest.

Thursday 13th October 2022

Friday 14th October 2022

Sat 15th & Sun 16th October 2022

Monday 17th October 2022

The Mexican National Guard attempt to arrest drug lord Ovidio Guzmán López, but are surprised when 700 cartel members launch an attack on the city of Culiacán, taking multiple hostages. Guzmán López is released to save the lives of civilians.

Tuesday 18th October 2022

The story goes that bartender Betsy Flanagan of Elmsford, New York serves her patrons drinks adorned with the tail feathers of a cockerel that she had stolen from her English neighbour. It is said that this is where the term cocktail originated.

Wednesday 19th October 2022

The Spanish ship *San Felipe* runs aground on Shikoku in Japan. An ill-judged remark by the ship's pilot, inferring that the Spanish sent missionaries ahead of their military to conquer a country, leads to the round-up and execution of 26 Christians by the Japanese.

Thursday 20th October 2022

On this day

1572

To rescue the city of Goes, besieged by Anglo-Dutch forces and threatening the city of Middelburg, 3,000 Spanish soldiers wade across the 15 mile wide Scheldt river with weapons held above their heads. The enemy troops, taken by surprise, retreat.

Friday 21st October 2022

On this day

1949

Aldous Huxley, author of *Brave New World*, writes to his former student George Orwell to congratulate him on the publication of *1984* and discusses whether his vision of a narco-hypnotic dystopia is more likely than Orwell's "boot-on-the-face" prophecy.

Sat 22nd & Sun 23rd October 2022

On this day

22nd October 1983

Two correctional officers are stabbed to death by inmates at USP Marion. This leads to calls for a new form of prison, designed to isolate dangerous inmates, and Marion becomes the first Supermax prison where inmates remain in their cells for 23 hours a day.

Monday 24th October 2022

63 year old Annie Edson Taylor becomes the first person to survive going over Niagara Falls in a barrel. She performed the stunt in hopes of gaining financial security, but never made much profit. She attributed the poor health of her later years to the stunt.

Tuesday 25th October 2022

The Zinoviev Letter is published in the Daily Mail, suggesting that Moscow's Comintern is working with the British Communist Party. The Labour Party, who sought trade with Moscow, thus lose the 1924 election. The letter has since been proved a forgery.

Wednesday 26th October 2022

Somali cook Ali Maow Maalin becomes the world's last case of naturally occurring smallpox. An aggressive programme of contact tracing and vaccination prevents further spread. The WHO now celebrate this date as the anniversary of smallpox's eradication.

Thursday 27th October 2022

Friday 28th October 2022

Sat 29th & Sun 30th October 2022

Monday 31st October 2022

Harry Houdini dies nine days after being punched in the stomach by student Jacques Price. It is possible that the blows did not directly cause his death, but instead that the pain prevented him from realising that he had appendicitis in time to be saved.

Tuesday 1st November 2022

Montreal Canadiens' goaltender Jacques Plante insists on wearing a homemade fibreglass mask after having his nose broken, despite his coach's protests. He goes on to develop new forms of mask, which are now mandatory for ice hockey goaltenders.

Wednesday 2nd November 2022

The Emu War begins as the Australian government send soldiers with machine guns to deal with the migratory birds, which were damaging farmers' crops. The War ends in failure as the emus prove too fast to target and able to absorb bullets.

Thursday 3rd November 2022

Friday 4th November 2022

Sat 5th & Sun 6th November 2022

Monday 7th November 2022

Jesús García Corona notices that train cars full of dynamite have caught fire while resting in the town of Nacozari in Mexico. He drives the train 3.7 miles before the cars explode, sparing the town, which has since been renamed Nacozari de García in his honour.

Tuesday 8th November 2022

The city of Venice, concerned that fire could destroy their wooden buildings, order all glassmakers to move to the island of Murano. Murano glass remains famous worldwide for its high quality and is one of Venice's most lucrative industries.

Wednesday 9th November 2022

Two British SIS agents are kidnapped by Nazis at Venlo, near the German-Dutch border. This led to the creation of the SOE spy network and Churchill's refusal to help German resistance for the rest of the war, as well as the invasion of the Netherlands.

Thursday 10th November 2022

On this day

1980

Journalist Dan Rather is trapped in a cab by Chicago taxi driver Gene Phillips, who alleges his fare was not paid. The police intervene upon seeing Rather shout for help through the window. Phillips is charged with disorderly conduct.

Friday 11th November 2022

On this day

1869

The Aboriginal Protection Act is brought into force in Australia, giving the government control over every aspect of indigenous people's lives, including their children. The policy of taking Aboriginal children from their families continues until the 1970s.

Sat 12th & Sun 13th November 2022

On this day

12th November 1970

An attempt by Oregon Highway Division to remove a sperm whale carcass with explosives goes awry when they use 450kg of dynamite rather than the recommended 3.8kg, resulting in blubber hitting onlookers, buildings and cars from a quarter-mile away.

Monday 14th November 2022

100 Mafiosi attend a meeting held by mobster Joseph Barbara in Apalachin, New York. The police, suspicious of so many expensive cars in the sleepy village, raid the house and arrest 60 bosses. This exposed the existence of a nationwide crime syndicate.

Tuesday 15th November 2022

Harry Turner becomes the first person to die from injuries sustained in American football when his spinal cord is severed by a bad tackle. His last words to his manager are "I'm satisfied, for we beat Peggy Parratt" referring to the captain of the rival team.

Wednesday 16th November 2022

An elevator at the John Hancock Center in Chicago falls 84 floors when a cable breaks. Firefighters must break through a wall in an underground garage to reach the six occupants, none of whom are injured.

Thursday 17th November 2022

On this day

1810

Sweden declares war against Great Britain, having been compelled to do so by France under threat of French invasion. No fighting occurs and Britain continues to conduct trade with Sweden. Peace was re-established by the Treaty of Orebro in 1812.

Friday 18th November 2022

On this day

1987

A lit match dropped on the wooden escalator at King's Cross station begins a small fire which, due to previously unknown trench effect, suddenly increases in intensity and engulfs the ticket hall. It is the first fatal fire on the London Underground.

Sat 19th & Sun 20th November 2022

On this day

20th November 1820

The whaling ship *Essex* is sunk by a sperm whale thousands of miles from South America's coast. The 20-man crew survive the sinking, but only 8 are found alive three months later. The event inspired Herman Melville's 1851 novel *Moby Dick* .

Monday 21st November 2022

Judas Maccabeus liberates Jerusalem from the Seleucid forces, the first step towards the city's complete independence, and restores the Temple of Jerusalem. The event is celebrated in the annual Jewish holiday of Hanukkah.

Tuesday 22nd November 2022

Black and mixed race crewmen of the Brazilian navy stage a mutiny against corporal punishment by white officers. Unable to sink the rebellious ships, the government agrees to ban corporal punishment, but many mutineers are later imprisoned.

Wednesday 23rd November 2022

Thespis wins an Athenian contest for best tragedy and becomes the first documented actor to play a character rather than himself. In recognition of the storytelling style he invented, modern theatre actors are referred to as thespians.

Thursday 24th November 2022

On this day

1971

A man known as D.B. Cooper hijacks Northwest Orient Flight 305, demands $200,000 and a parachute, and then leaps out of the plane. He and the money have never been seen again, and Cooper's true identity has never been uncovered.

Friday 25th November 2022

On this day

1120

The *White Ship* sinks off Normandy, claiming 299 lives including Henry I's son and heir William. This began a succession war between Henry's daughter Matilda and nephew Stephen, the latter of whom had disembarked the *White Ship* before it set sail.

Sat 26th & Sun 27th November 2022

On this day

27th November 1809

Theodore Hook, a notorious practical joker, writes thousands of letters requesting deliveries to 54 Berners Street. The home of Mrs Tottenham is thus besieged by every form of tradesperson in London, requiring police presence to disperse the crowd.

Monday 28th November 2022

After two postponements, the first motor car race is held in Chicago. The winner is Frank Duryea with a time of 10 hours and 23 minutes, and only one other car completes the 54 mile course. Commercial production of automobiles begins only a year later.

Tuesday 29th November 2022

Upon hearing his guilty verdict for war crimes during the 1990s and impending 20 year prison sentence, Bosnian-Croat general Slobodan Praljak drinks poison inside a courtroom of The Hague. He dies in a nearby hospital at the age of 72.

Wednesday 30th November 2022

Dr Francisco Javier de Balmis and his group set off from Galicia on a three year voyage to bring the smallpox vaccine to South America and Asia, successfully protecting millions of people in approximately 14 countries.

Thursday 1st December 2022

Friday 2nd December 2022

Sat 3rd & Sun 4th December 2022

Monday 5th December 2022

1945

Five torpedo bombers vanish over the Bermuda Triangle during a US Navy training exercise, followed by the seaplane sent to search for them. The long-standing mythos of the Bermuda Triangle is born from this incident.

Tuesday 6th December 2022

1956

Against the backdrop of the Hungarian Revolution, the USSR and Hungary meet for a water polo match at the Melbourne Olympics. Both teams taunt and attack each other throughout. The match is stopped when blood is drawn, with Hungary winning 4-0.

Wednesday 7th December 2022

1987

David Burke is able to bypass airport security using his USAir credentials, despite being fired, and crashes Pacific Southwest 1771 after killing his former boss. As a result, airline staff are now subject to the same security measures as ordinary passengers.

Thursday 8th December 2022

On this day

1504

Ahmad ibn Abi Jum'ah issues the Oran fatwa, permitting Muslims in Spain to outwardly conform to Christianity, an action normally forbidden in Islamic law, to survive attempts to forcibly convert them. The fatwa applies only to Spain.

Friday 9th December 2022

On this day

1868

The first traffic lights are erected outside the Houses of Parliament, using semaphore arms like a railway crossing for daylight and manually operated coloured gas lamps for night. The lamps explode on 2 January 1869, taking the traffic lights out of commission.

Sat 10th & Sun 11th December 2022

On this day

11th December 1718

Charles XII of Sweden is killed by a projectile whilst inspecting his troops during the Siege of Fredriksten in Norway. The Swedish army immediately calls off the attack, ending the Great Northern War and the imperial era of Sweden.

Monday 12th December 2022

54 Japanese fighter planes raid Batangas Base in the Philippines. In response six Filipino pilots take to the skies and engage them, successfully preventing them from reaching Lipa Airfield. Only one of the Filipino pilots is lost in the fight.

Tuesday 13th December 2022

Pope Celestine V resigns from his post, only five months after being elected pope and a week after confirming the right of the pope to abdicate, in order to return to his previous life as a hermetic monk. He is instead imprisoned to prevent a threat to the new pope Boniface VIII.

Wednesday 14th December 2022

A conspiracy by Emperor Wenzong to kill the powerful eunuchs fails when a gust of wind lifts a screen to reveal armed soldiers, and the eunuchs kill all but the emperor. For the rest of the Tang dynasty, the eunuchs hold total power over government.

Thursday 15th December 2022

1836

A fire at the US Patent Office destroys approximately 9,957 patent records and 7,000 invention models. As a result unique numbers were applied to patents, making it easier to find them, and multiple copies were required to ensure any losses could be restored.

Friday 16th December 2022

1937

Bank robbers Theodore Cole and Ralph Roe escape from Alcatraz Prison. It is believed they did not survive the swim to shore, but their remains have never been found and the possibility of their success challenges Alcatraz's escape-proof reputation.

Sat 17th & Sun 18th December 2022

17th December 2010

Tunisian street vendor Mohamed Bouazizi self-immolates in protest at municipal harassment. Public anger after his death causes the Tunisian president to step down, and inspires the Arab Spring protests against other autocratic regimes.

Monday 19th December 2022

The unpopular Sir William Lyne is appointed Prime Minister of the Australian interim government as he is the Premier of the country's most populous region, but is unable to convince any politicians to join his government and resigns five days later.

Tuesday 20th December 2022

King Richard I is captured by Leopold V of Austria. He is later ransomed for 150,000 marks by Holy Roman Emperor Henry VI. Richard's brother John offers 80,000 marks for his continued captivity, but this offer is refused and Richard is released in 1194.

Wednesday 21st December 2022

Arthur Wynne creates a diamond-shaped word puzzle for the *Fun* section of the *New York World*. It is initially named a Word-Cross, but a typing error several weeks later changes the name to Cross-Word, which it has been called ever since.

Thursday 22nd December 2022

On this day

1944

At the Battle of the Bulge, US general Anthony McAuliffe receives an order from the Germans to surrender and responds "Nuts!" This is the official reply given to the Germans and, upon expressing confusion, they are told "In plain English? Go to hell."

Friday 23rd December 2022

On this day

1972

16 of the 28 survivors from Uruguayan Air Force Flight 571, which crashed in the Andes on 13 October, are found after two of the group hiked into Chile to find help. They had been stranded in the mountains for 72 days and resorted to cannibalism to survive.

Sat 24th & Sun 25th December 2022

On this day

24th December 820

Byzantine Emperor Leo V is killed in the Hagia Sophia by assassins disguised as choir members. His successor, Michael II, was in prison at the time and Leo had hidden the key on his person. A blacksmith could not be found and Michael was crowned still in shackles.

Monday 26th December 2022

The Boston Red Sox sell Babe Ruth to the New York Yankees. Previously one of the most successful baseball teams, the Red Sox fail to win a championship for the next century as the Yankees become one of baseball's greatest teams.

Tuesday 27th December 2022

A month after laying siege to the Jasna Góra monastery in Poland, Swedish forces withdraw. 310 monks have successfully held off an army of 3,200. The monastery is the only Polish stronghold that is not captured by the Swedish.

Wednesday 28th December 2022

Corrie ten Boom, whose family were caught sheltering Jews in the Netherlands, is released from Ravensbruck concentration camp due to a clerical error. Upon her return to Amsterdam, she once again opens her home to those in need of shelter.

Thursday 29th December 2022

1503

With the help of Italian reinforcements, the Spanish forces win a decisive victory over the French at the Battle of Garigliano by secretly building a bridge across the river and forcing a retreat. Spanish supremacy in the Kingdom of Naples lasts for centuries.

Friday 30th December 2022

On this day

1903

Over 602 people are killed in a fire during a sold-out matinee performance at the Iroquois Theatre in Chicago. Advertised as fireproof, in fact only three doors could be found and unlocked, and many people were killed in dead ends after mistaking scenery for exits.

Sat 31st & Sun 1st January 2023

On this day

1st January 404

According to historian Theodoret, Saint Telemachus attempts to stop a gladiatorial fight and is stoned to death by the crowd. Impressed by the monk, Emperor Honorius declares a ban on gladiatorial fights, making this the last to take place in Rome.

NOTES

NOTES

2023 CALENDAR

JANUARY

M	T	W	T	F	S	S
						1
2	3	4	5	6	7	8
9	10	11	12	13	14	15
16	17	18	19	20	21	22
23	24	25	26	27	28	29
30	31					

FEBRUARY

M	T	W	T	F	S	S
		1	2	3	4	5
6	7	8	9	10	11	12
13	14	15	16	17	18	19
20	21	22	23	24	25	26
27	28					

MARCH

M	T	W	T	F	S	S
		1	2	3	4	5
6	7	8	9	10	11	12
13	14	15	16	17	18	19
20	21	22	23	24	25	26
27	28	29	30	31		

APRIL

M	T	W	T	F	S	S
					1	2
3	4	5	6	7	8	9
10	11	12	13	14	15	16
17	18	19	20	21	22	23
24	25	26	27	28	29	30

MAY

M	T	W	T	F	S	S
1	2	3	4	5	6	7
8	9	10	11	12	13	14
15	16	17	18	19	20	21
22	23	24	25	26	27	28
29	30	31				

JUNE

M	T	W	T	F	S	S
			1	2	3	4
5	6	7	8	9	10	11
12	13	14	15	16	17	18
19	20	21	22	23	24	25
26	27	28	29	30		

JULY

M	T	W	T	F	S	S
					1	2
3	4	5	6	7	8	9
10	11	12	13	14	15	16
17	18	19	20	21	22	23
24	25	26	27	28	29	30
31						

AUGUST

M	T	W	T	F	S	S
	1	2	3	4	5	6
7	8	9	10	11	12	13
14	15	16	17	18	19	20
21	22	23	24	25	26	27
28	29	30	31			

SEPTEMBER

M	T	W	T	F	S	S
				1	2	3
4	5	6	7	8	9	10
11	12	13	14	15	16	17
18	19	20	21	22	23	24
25	26	27	28	29	30	

OCTOBER

M	T	W	T	F	S	S
						1
2	3	4	5	6	7	8
9	10	11	12	13	14	15
16	17	18	19	20	21	22
23	24	25	26	27	28	29
30	31					

NOVEMBER

M	T	W	T	F	S	S
		1	2	3	4	5
6	7	8	9	10	11	12
13	14	15	16	17	18	19
20	21	22	23	24	25	26
27	28	29	30			

DECEMBER

M	T	W	T	F	S	S
				1	2	3
4	5	6	7	8	9	10
11	12	13	14	15	16	17
18	19	20	21	22	23	24
25	26	27	28	29	30	31

Printed in Great Britain
by Amazon